A TIME
TO BE SILENT

What *"Taking Time To Be Still"*
Will Do For You

Jesus Himself drew near
Lu 24.15

Anne Sandberg.

i

Be Still and know J Am God

From a Painting by 9 year old
Dwanette Garr
(used by permission)

A TIME

TO BE SILENT

What *"Taking Time To Be Still"*
Will Do For You

Anne Sandberg

A TIME TO BE SILENT
What *"Taking Time To Be Still"* Will Do For You

Copyright © 1994

by

Anne Sandberg

Printed in the United States of America

Published by

Abel II Publishing
P.O. Box 15486
San Diego, California 92175
U.S.A.

Library of Congress Catalog Card Number: 94-70899
ISBN 0-9624398-9-4   7.95

To Bob and Nina Lyon

who introduced me to

silent prayer.

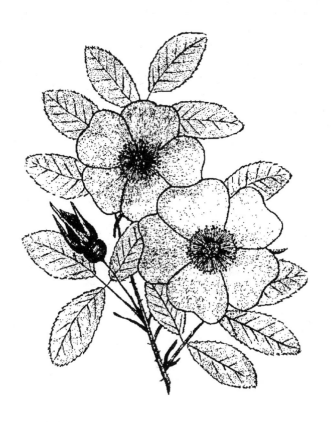

Make me like you, Lord,

Make me like you.

You are a servant.

Make me one too.

Lord, I am willing.

Do what you must do

To make me like you, Lord.

Make me like you.

by Sabra Ann Fox
(used by permission)

To every thing there is a season, . . .
. . . a time to keep silence, . . .

(Ecclesiastes 3:1-,-7-)

Be still and know that J am God: . . .

(Psalm 46:10-)

CONTENTS

Ch. #	Title	Page

I come to the garden alone
While the dew is still on the roses,
And the voice I hear,
Falling on my ear,
The Son of God discloses.

And He walks with me,
And He talks with me,
And He tells me I am His own
And the joy we share
As we tarry there,
None other has ever known.

There are delights which the heart may enjoy in the awesome presence of God which cannot find expression in language; they belong to the unutterable element in Christian experience. Not many enjoy them because not many know they can.

The above is from A. W. Tozer's *Root of the Righteous*

INTRODUCTION

— by Martha Jacobson Bauer
Retired A/G missionary of 41
years in Nigeria, West Africa

Anne Sandberg and I have been friends for 65 years. She received Christ at about the same time as my conversion when we were both attending high school. Joanne Modder, also a student, was used of God to bring each of us to a decision. Joanne's church, Peniel Tabernacle in Kenosha, Wisconsin, became our church home.

Ann and I grew in lovership with Jesus as our early pastors (all associated with the Faith Homes in Zion, Illinois) nurtured us. We were told that the meeting began when we met with the Lord. Often people came early to the services just to enjoy the presence of Jesus. When one entered the first big door of the church into a small vestibule, one just naturally lowered one's voice for it was truly a house of prayer. A sign on the second door to the main sanctuary read, ". . . The LORD *is* in his holy temple: let all the earth keep silence before him." (Habakkuk 2:-20)

On entering the auditorium one soon became aware of a soft murmur of praise and worship. The ministers on the platform were on their knees as were a scattering of people throughout the building—all in sacred communion often with their arms raised. Eventually those kneeling at the altar and elsewhere would find a seat and sit—either reading the Bible or in an obvious attitude of waiting to hear from God. Different ones would lead out in a chorus, a prayer or read from the Bible under the direction of the Holy Spirit.

God was there!

As an unconverted teenager I was awed by the radiant faces of the worshipers. God was real to them. It brought a strong conviction of sin and led me into complete surrender of my life to my seeking Lover-God. I soon learned to enjoy Him for Himself alone, not just what He did for me.

Anne came often to our farm on the north side of Kenosha. We watched her grow spiritually like a delicate unfolding rose. You will greatly benefit by letting her lead you into the beautiful garden of prayer and worship where our Savior awaits and opens the gates.

When I first read Anne's manuscript, it disturbed me that she had been delayed in getting it printed as I felt that the church of Jesus Christ greatly needed it. I know I did! In this present age of nervous tension, stress, rush and business, even among Christians, this book will be of value in reminding us that "there is a place of quiet rest, near to the heart of God."

A TIME TO BE SILENT is not another book on prayer. It is about communion. In prayer we are giving attention to our needs or the needs of others; in communion we are silently paying attention to Jesus—listening to Him, loving Him. Anne reminds us that our Lord is always waiting, longing for our response to His invitation: "Come . . . I will give you rest . . . Come ye apart . . . Come away my beloved.."

The most loving act of a person to his or her mate is to listen to them, giving full attention. The same is true in expressing love to an older person or to a small child. Our highest expression of love to God is to take time to be silent before Him in loving, relaxed attentiveness. Learning to enjoy God's presence now, gives a little prelude to what heaven is like.

In Joni Eareckson Tada's book, *A QUIET PLACE IN A CRAZY WORLD*, she says "God meets us anywhere . . . and everywhere. There is never a place where He is not. He waits in every room we're about to enter. He stands quietly in the back of every elevator before we step through the doors. He lingers around the bend of every path we will walk. . . . God is there for you . . . so draw near to Him. . . ."

May you hear our Lord calling you as you read *A TIME TO BE SILENT*.

If Jesus delays His coming and I live, I hope to sell enough books just to pay the expense of printing. Then I would like to give *A TIME TO BE SILENT* to over four thousand of my Nigerian brothers and sisters who are so faithfully ministering in Nigeria without the impact of spiritual books.

NOTE:
Help me get this project moving by ordering books through me at:

9818 Estrella Drive
Spring Valley, CA 91977

Please see the order form on page 109 for price ($7.95), ordering information and quantity discounts.

My first book, *HEY, THIS IS FUN!*, is also available for the same price. It is full of adventure and Christian victory from my 41 years missionary ministry in Nigeria, West Africa. It will help make missionaries out of your young people. It, too, should be in every library.

THE ANSWER

When for a purpose I had prayed
    And prayed and prayed,
Until my words seemed worn and bare
    With arduous use,
And I had knocked and asked and knocked
    And asked again,
Yet with all my fervor and persistence,
    It brought no hope.

I paused to give my weary brain a rest
    And ceased my anxious human cry.
In that still moment after self
    Had tried and failed,
There came a glorious vision
    Of God's power,
And lo, my prayer was answered
    In that very hour!

STILL

If you stand very still in the heart of a woods,
You will hear many wonderful things:
The snap of a twig and the wind in the trees.
If you stand very still in the turmoil of life
And you wait for the voice from within,
You'll be led down the quiet ways of wisdom and peace.
In a mad world of chaos and din,
If you stand very still and you hold to your faith,
You will draw from the silence the things that you need:
Hope and courage and strength for your task.

—Above poems by Sabra Ann Fox
(used by permission)

A Moment Well Spent

by Mr. Jack Hamm

Chapter 1
How It Began

Called by any euphemistic name— bachelor girl, unclaimed blessing, liberated woman—I still felt the same. I was an *Old Maid*— something I fervently didn't want to be!

"Why should I?" I demanded of the Lord. "After all, before I accepted Christ, I had plenty of boy friends."

Before I accepted Christ. That meant when I was a high school senior of seventeen—homework on weekdays, dates on weekends. First, there was Leslie to take me dancing. I loved that. Afterwards hamburgers and cokes. Fun. But Leslie was five years older and talked of marriage, and I was enjoying life too much to settle down yet.

Next came George, who quoted from: *The Rubaiyat* by Omar Kyayyam. But he drank too much.

Then Freddie, who liked the movies.

But it was always the same, whether it was Freddie, George or Leslie—or someone else. After a date I'd ponder, "Is this all there is to life? Dates, marriage, family, middle age, old age—joining that endless stream of life flowing into death?" It all seemed so futile!

Monday morning. Back in school, studying hard. And there was Joanne, my new friend. Between classes she gave me wisps of hope, talking about Jesus and a purpose in life. It ended with my accepting Christ and joining her gospel church. Lots of young people there, many activities. Hummmmm. Nice.

Yes, I loved Jesus, but still put a high priority on fun, only now in a Christian setting.

Oh, those church picnics! Cavorting on the beach, imbibing cokes, home baked beans, chocolate cake. Then a short service after lunch and more fun. At night it would be campfire, holding hands with the current boyfriend while singing gospel songs. Boys and fun plus the gospel. Perfect!

Then came graduation from high school, followed by Christian college for many of our group. "If you want a husband, go to a Christian college." Nobody said it aloud, but we girls knew that's the way it was; so I planned to go next year and to become a minister's wife.

But my plans were disrupted by my parents' divorce, and I was now needed to help my mother and two younger brothers. Disappointed, I began my life of "sacrifice." As secretary in a law office, I contributed much of my salary toward family needs. At first it wasn't that bad. College friends returned on holidays and it was exciting seeing them.

However, during the second year I noticed subtle changes. While they had made new friends, I had become less important to them.

"School's great," they would exult. "When are you coming."

"Next year, for sure," I replied. But when the time came, I just couldn't walk out on my mother and brothers.

At the church there were changes too. The next generation of youths were too young for me and I felt lonely. As I became active in church work, older folks approvingly called me "faithful Anne." But they didn't know my inner struggles—or did my sad eyes betray me?

At weddings my heart crumpled. When friends patted me and smiled, "You're next, Anne," I'd reply, "Perhaps," pretending light-heartedness. But my heart cried bitterly, "Who could I marry?" The only bachelors in our small church were: One simple-minded young fellow, an illiterate middle-aged man, two older widowers and a bearded old man who was fond of me. Slim pickin's!

When I turned thirty, a close younger friend got married and I was her attendant. Late that night, I dropped my limp bouquet on the dresser and stared into the mirror. The face I saw was no longer fresh and dewy; the eyes were dull, the expression sad. "Hopeless old maid," I thought and wept uncontrolledly.

When I became still, from deep within I heard that soft, sweet sound, like the cooing of a dove, and something vaguely stirred in my heart. Hadn't I heard that voice for years? It was not a call to sacrifice, but a call to Himself. But I always closed my heart.

Strange, piteous, futile thing! Perhaps I
was afraid, lest having Him, I must
have nought beside.

—from Thompson's *The Hound Of Heaven*

During those years of struggle, I had become a
serious student of the Bible. Here again I heard the
Lord's call—in the Psalms of David:

In thy presence is fulness of joy.
(Psalm 16.11)

In the story of Mary sitting at Jesus' feet; in the
example of Jesus Himself:

I delight to do thy will, O my God.
(Psalm 40.8)

I heard His call in the devotion of spiritual
people, particularly my friend Joanne, who was
now the wife of our pastor, aglow with love for
Jesus.

I longed to be like her. So I began to pray
earnestly, desperately—not for a husband, but that
I would be happy without one. Preachers said,
"Jesus is the answer; He satisfies the longing heart.
He is all you need."

I knew it had to be so. I wanted to experience it,
prove it to myself, to the world, to the devil—that I
could be happy with Jesus alone. Otherwise, Chris-
tianity would be meaningless.

Years of prayer dragged by. Eventually my
brothers grew up, and I was free. By now I was too
old for school or marriage. I had run into several
unattached men I had known in the world who
wanted dates, but I refused to be unequally yoked

with unbelievers. So I kept praying for the victorious experience I longed for.

It came in an unexpected way—not through praying, but when I stopped praying.

When I was thirty-one, I moved in with a young minister and wife to assist in youth work. As we prayed together every morning, I began to notice something. I was always petitioning; they began prayer with silence, faces upturned, worshipping. With awe I watched their radiant countenances, heard them murmur, "I love you Jesus; you are wonderful." Not only did they love Jesus, but they seemed to be **in love** with Him!

One day the minister asked, "Anne, you know how to pray, but have you ever learned to silently wait on God?" I hardly knew what he meant. "Do you want to learn?" The hunger in my eyes was his answer, and he gave me a small volume by Andrew Murray, *Waiting On God.*

"Read a little, then be silent, keeping your attention on Jesus," he instructed. "When your mind wanders, read a little more, then look at Jesus again. Get really acquainted with Him. Be with Him."

The next day at personal devotions, I tried but was surprised to find it wasn't easy. My mind continually wandered. I straightened a crooked picture, picked a thread off the rug, thought of my correspondence.

I read a few more sentences, turned my mind back to the Lord. The hour was a chore, but I kept trying, encouraged by the minister's words and example. Later he gave me: *Practice of the Presence of God*, by Brother Lawrence, and later other books on the inward life.

Slowly, I began to enter a new spiritual dimension. Like a flower turned toward the sun, my heart responded to Jesus' love. After about a year, I began looking forward to that time of sitting at the feet of Jesus. The pangs of loneliness became less frequent, less painful; envy of married couples decreased.

In short, I was getting my eyes off myself, paying attention to Jesus, and finding Him exceedingly lovely. One day as I was still before God, I realized that something beautiful had happened to me. His presence so filled my being that I could say from my heart,

> Whom have I in heaven but Thee? There is none upon earth that I desire beside Thee. (Psalm 73:25)

I wept with joy. Oh, how lovely He was! He was all I needed, all I wanted, and He was wonderful, wonderful! I was now thirty-three and life was just beginning. Faithfully as before, I continued having devotions, including times of silence. I also continued my involvement in Christian work, but now with a heart aglow with love for Jesus.

Eventually I returned to my home area around Kenosha, Wisconsin to help in Vacation Bible School. I was a radiant, thirty-five. To my surprise, three Christian gentlemen began courting me. (I didn't think there were any older eligibles around.) Strangely, I wasn't too impressed because Jesus was now the center of my life and everything else was secondary.

I did pray about these three and chose Gil. Our marriage was singularly happy, blessed later with one daughter born to us, and another—a foster daughter. Despite the joy of being wife and mother, I still found my highest happiness in Jesus.

Nothing else was as wonderful as my quiet hour, sitting at the feet of Jesus, my Beloved. Of course there were testings, heartaches, spiritual dryness. But always He lifted me; always there remained an abiding love for Jesus.

And now that I am a widow and alone again, I still say:

> I delight to do thy will, O my God: . . . .
> (Psalm 40:8-)

For:

> . . . in thy presence *is* fulness of joy; at thy right hand *there are* pleasures forevermore.   (Psalm 16:-11)

NOTE: This Chapter 1 was Published as an Article in *Aglow Magazine* Issue #28

Chapter 2
Loving Jesus

Whom having not seen, ye love; . . .
                    (1 Peter 1:8-)

One of the greatest of all human needs is to love and be loved. But multitudes are deprived: the divorced, the widowed, the single, the unhappily married, even many children and young people. Most of them are looking in the wrong directions for love and fulfillment.

Unattached persons feel that acquiring a mate will bring happiness; the childless couple think a baby will do it; the unhappily married person longs for a different mate.

But even if conditions were ideal: the marriage happy, children perfect, in-laws great, material possessions adequate, status up to par—still there would come a sense of emptiness and incompleteness.

What is the reason? Why do human relationships, material possessions and honors, even among Christians, often end in disappointment; or if remaining intact, never bring the expected happiness and satisfaction?

The reason is that in essence, we are not **body** but **spirit,** with yearnings and affinities for The Eternal. St. Augustine rightly said,

> Thou hast made us for Thyself and the
> heart is restless until it rests in Thee.

The problem with us is not that we love people and places and things too much, but that we don't love Jesus enough. When He becomes the center of life, everything else takes its proper place and proportion. Therefore, loving Jesus is one of the most stabilizing forces in life.

That was why Jesus declared the first and great commandment to be,

> . . . Thou shalt love the Lord thy God
> with all thy heart, and with all thy soul,
> and with all thy mind.   (Matt. 22:-37)

In attaching so much importance to such total love to Himself, Jesus laid down the foundation for the fulfillment of all the longings of the spirit of man.

Jean Pigott expressed this in the poem:

> [1]Simply trusting thee, Lord Jesus
> I behold thee as thou art;
> And thy love so pure, so changeless
> Satisfies my heart;
> Satisfies its deepest longings,
> Meets, supplies its every need.
> Compasseth me round with blessings,
> Thine is love indeed.

The basic need of man is met at conversion, at which time he often experiences the first love, which is the awakening of the heart to the wonder of Jesus Himself. But this love must be constantly nourished or it will fade, and Jesus will be obliged to say,

> I have somewhat against thee, because
> thou hast left Thy first love." (Rev. 2:4)

Many converts never do experience that kind of relationship to Jesus but simply accept Him in a sort of evangelically correct mental way. So we find dedicated Christians who love the Word of the Lord but who have an inadequate personal affection for the Lord of the Word.

Christians know that Jesus included in that first and great commandment the love of others as the second half. We are also aware that He defined love as the keeping of His commandments. But that still does not rule out the fact that the Lord desires our **affections** as well. Should not the bride of Christ be in love with her Bridegroom?

Ask any bride and groom what love is. Is it an intellectual appraisal of each other's virtues? A commitment to be faithful? Or a promise to honor and obey? Yes, all this is included. But is that what puts the glow on the face of the bridal **pair,**—the great delight in being together?

Lovers could very well relate to the rapturous song of Bernard of Clairvaux:

> [2]Jesus., the very thought of thee
> With sweetness fills my breast;
>   But sweeter far thy face to see
>   And in thy presence rest.

It is significant that many. contemporary scripture choruses center on worship and love to Jesus. Surely this indicates a trend toward a desire in many for a deeper love relationship with Jesus.

GOD'S NEED TO LOVE AND BE LOVED

But there is another side to this. Not only does man need to give and receive love, but God does as well. This insight was given to Lucie Christine, a devout nineteenth century Christian. One day she lamented her inability to minister to the poor because she was so busy with her family of five children. The Lord Jesus then said to her,

> I am the first among the poor of this world, first among the most forsaken. I am the Great Abandoned One. And none think of Me.

God is love. He is so full of love that He must impart it. To whom can He impart it: to the vast universe which He created—the sun, moon, stars and innumerable galaxies, the angels, the planet earth and the animals and birds upon it? Out of this list only the angels would be responsive, but they are not sufficient. Therefore God made man like unto Himself with whom He could intimately fellowship.

The entire story of God's relationship with mankind is a story of love. Often in the Old Testament God is represented as Jehovah-husband and Israel as the wife. In the New Testament, Jesus is the Bridegroom and the church is the Bride. That love relationship will be climaxed in heaven at the marriage supper of the Lamb.

But love must be reciprocal. God would never be satisfied to be forever loving us and not receiving our love in return. God is love and He wants love in return. He wants the praise and adoration and worship of loving hearts.

Communion, fellowship with Himself, is what God desires—our tiny thimbleful of love measured against His ocean of love. Yet He wants it all.

The Song of Solomon gives us a Biblical example of what may seem extravagant displays of mutual love. Since the very nature and essence of God's being is love, it is inevitable that any contact with Him will evoke a response of love.

Is there a way to restore the first love, or to keep from losing it in the first place? Is there a way to enable one to have more frequent times of experiencing the presence of God and to bring us into greater love for Jesus Himself?

Yes, there is. Briefly, it is the way which Jesus commended in Mary, who sat at His feet. It is learning to be still before the Lord, being with Him, waiting quietly, worshipfully in His presence, looking into His face.

As we do this, we begin to develop a love relationship with Jesus. We learn the joy of living in His presence, for,

> In thy presence is fulness of joy, at thy right hand there are pleasures forever-more.   (Psalm 16:11)

We will also discover that no matter what our lot in life, what the struggles, the sufferings, the loneliness—through this intimate fellowship with

Jesus we can become so complete and fulfilled that we can honestly say,

> Whom have I in heaven but thee; there
> is none upon earth that I desire beside
> thee. (Psalm 73:25)

And there are "side effects." We become more relaxed outwardly, physically. We are more restful inwardly, more serene and tranquil. We begin to enjoy the fulfilling, satisfying experience of living in the love and presence of God.

Chapter 3
What This Book Is About

[1]Oh Jesus, blessed Redeemer
Sent from the heart of God;
Hold us who wait before Thee
Near to the heart of God.
                    — Cleland B. McAfee

From the beginning of time there have always been those who learned the secrets of that kind of relationship with God. It is the way which Jesus commended in Mary, who sat at His feet. It is the reason John was called "the disciple whom Jesus loved,"—he who leaned on Jesus' bosom.

In seeking an appropriate name for this practice—waiting on God, contemplation, silent worship—we would perhaps feel most comfortable with the word **communion,** meaning intimate fellowship with God. John the Beloved puts it like this:

> . . . truly our fellowship *is* with the
> Father, and with His Son Jesus Christ.
> (1 John 1:-3)

At this point, some will say, "Oh, you are talking about prayer." No, I am not—not in the sense commonly understood.

But, don't we have fellowship with God when we pray?

We may or we may not. Often we do not. In prayer we are chiefly aware of ourselves and our needs and the needs of others. In communion we are paying attention to the Lord Jesus Himself.

In prayer we speak to God either orally or mentally. In communion we are silent. In supplication some people pace the floor; in communion the body is relaxed. In prayer the mind is active; in communion it is still. In prayer we are occupied with ourselves and our needs or the needs of others. In communion we are deliberately centering our attention on God alone. Instead of His gifts or favors, we are seeking just Himself. Communion is cultivating a love relationship with God, developing an intimate knowledge, having personal fellowship with Him.

Those familiar with Scripture know that vocal or mental prayer is enjoined upon Christians and should be an integral part of our walk with God.

> Praying always with all prayer and supplication . . . (Eph. 6:18-) and,
> Pray without ceasing. (1 Thess. 5:17)

However, not everyone is aware that silent communion, in which one stills the activities of the mind and centers the spirit upon God, is also commanded in Scripture. Consider (Zechariah 2:13-):

> Be silent, O all flesh, before the Lord: . . .

> Also (Psalm 46:10-),

> Be still, and know that I *am* God: . . . .

In the Lord's prayer Jesus tells us that before we begin asking, we are to hallow His name, which implies an act of worship. Many other Scriptures speak of stillness.

Since this form of silent communion is recommended in the Scripture, why don't we hear about it in our churches? A simple answer would be, "Because most ministers themselves don't practice it." If they did, they would understand its value and advocate it.

Since the early days of the church, this kind of communion had been very much a part of its practice and was encouraged, commended, engaged in and written about by both clergy and laymen. After the 18th century this art largely faded out.

One reason was that the church became increasingly intellectual and institutionalized, leaving no place for a practice which brought people into such great intimacy with God.

Another great factor in the loss of the practice of silent prayer is that from the 18th century to the present there has been a change of emphasis.

In a time of great soul-winning efforts by the evangelical segment of the church, and vigorous social action by the more formal churches, the nurture of the inner life seemed to the church leaders and theologians to be unnecessary and obsolete.

Hence, while paying attention to the needs of the sinner, they have largely ignored or neglected the needs of the saint. Yet the pressures of modern living are taking their toll on both sinner and saint.

Thousands of the unconverted seek help in Eastern meditation. But what is being done for Christians who are longing for greater inner rest, a deeper walk with God and closer fellowship with Him?

We hope that the church will restore, to its original place of importance, the practice of this form of prayer. David cried,

> Oh God, thou art my God; early will I seek thee; my soul thirsteth for thee, my flesh longeth for thee in a dry and thirsty land, where no water is: To see thy power and thy glory, so as I have seen thee in the sanctuary.   (Psalm 63:1-2)

He is expressing the innate, though often hidden cry of the soul which is ever seeking close fellowship with God.

The fact is, also, that it is really God Himself who is constantly wooing and pursuing us. He is knocking at the heart's door of saints and sinners alike, either for an original entrance or for a deeper and more habitual entrance.   (Reference: Rev. 3.20)

So then, communion with God is simply stopping long enough for Him to catch up with us!

This longing of man and God for fellowship is as old as time. In the garden of Eden, God and man had perfect communion and fellowship. Even after the fall, there remained in man a God-inbreathed affinity for God, Himself.

Chapter 4

The Allegory of Adam

It was a few hours before sundown. While Eve sewed tiny garments from soft lambskin, Adam stood in the doorway absorbing the glow of the setting sun. A restlessness impelled him toward a wooded hill nearby, where he sat, musing.

Far to the north lay the garden from which he and his wife had been expelled. Eden—beautiful beyond anything which now surrounded him! But it was not the *place,* it was the *close fellowship* he missed the most.

Regularly, in the cool of the day God would come, to instruct or to converse with them or to silently enjoy sweet fellowship.

Sighing, Adam remembered how immersed he had been in that wonderful atmosphere which always attended God's presence, and how he had felt peace, wholeness, joy, and above all an overwhelming sense of love and security. It had been bliss, pure bliss.

Would he ever again experience that degree of happiness and companionship? Oblivious to all around him, Adam centered his whole being on that One whom he had known so intimately in the Garden of Eden.

As he waited quietly, eyes closed, face up-turned, he became aware that God had drawn nigh. Peace settled over his body, his mind, his spirit. A radiance, a glory seemed to stream down upon him like warm sunshine. God's presence, though un-seen, was ineffably wonderful.

Just before darkness fell, he arose, rapt in that glorious Presence and turned homeward.

In the days that followed his new encounter with God, Adam found himself being more gentle to his wife, more understanding. And that deeply buried resentment against her because she had first hearkened to the Tempter became less and less acute.

One evening, after Adam had returned from his now regular trysts with God, Eve asked him why he was so different. In hushed tones, Adam told her. And Eve, listening in awe, determined that she too would take moments in her day to thus silently commune with God.

So "the secret" was passed down from generation to generation. Among those who heard it was Enoch, the seventh from Adam, of whom it is written,

> . . . he walked with God and he was not,
> for God took him.   (Genesis 5:24)

Then there was Noah, the great grandson of Enoch, who also walked with God.

The Bible mentions others like-minded, among them, Abraham. We are not told what factors con-stituted this "walk with God." We can be sure that each of these men lived righteously, prayed and sought God. I would like to believe that they also understood the value of being still before God as a means to closer communion with Him.

Although there are previous references to this mode of prayer, the first explicit mention in the Old Testament is in the account of Isaac,

> . . . who went out to meditate and bow
> down *in prayer* in the open country in
> the evening . . .
> (Genesis 24:-63-) [Amplified Bible]

The next reference is in the story of Elijah on Mt. Horeb. (1 Kings 19:11-13) After the great wind and earthquake and fire, God came in a "still, small voice." Awed, Elijah wrapped his face in his mantle and stood before the Lord. Had he been busily engaged in vocal prayer, the prophet would not have heard that soft voice.

Other Bible men who spoke of this stillness were David, Isaiah and Habakkuk. Among the many references I will quote four:

In Psalm 46:10-, David wrote,
> Be still and know that I am God: . . . .

Isaiah said, in Isa. 30:-7,
> . . . Their strength is to sit still.

And again in Isaiah 30:-15-,
> . . . In returning and rest shall ye be
> saved; in quietness and confidence
> shall be your strength . . .

Habakkuk said, in Hab. 2:20,
> But the Lord is in His holy temple; let
> all the earth keep silence before Him.

God was so concerned about receiving worship and being ministered to and blessed that a number of Levites were appointed to be in the temple day and night to praise and bless the Lord. Doubtless much of the praise was audible. But in the Hebrew one of the words for praise is *baruch*, which means silent adoration. It is quite conceivable that after a period of audible worship, the Levites sensed such a great presence of God that they simply remained in silent awe and adoration, perhaps on their knees with hands raised. And in 2 Chronicles 5:14 we read that the priests were not able to minister because of the unusual presence of God.

From Enoch and David in the Old Testament to Mary and John in the New Testament, we learn of those who walked in close fellowship with God.

Within the various movements of the church, from its beginning until now, God always had His lovers. Throughout church history there were always those who responded to the call of God to the inner sanctuary where He dwells—among the best known being the early Quakers. Their desire was to walk with God in loving, intimate communion.

They are the ones who have learned that:

> [1]There is a place of quiet rest
> Near to the heart of God—
> A place where we our Savior meet
> Near to the heart of God.
> —Cleland B. McAfee

One of the best ways to enter into this life of intimacy with God is the practice of silent communion. But the ability to sit still before the Lord does not come automatically. It is a spiritual art which must be learned and then practiced until it becomes easy and natural.

The first requirement to learn is a determination to do so. Nothing substitutes for private devotions: neither meetings, nor Bible study classes, nor religious TV programs, nor cassette tapes, nor spiritual books. We must take time, make time to be alone with God.

Having made this decision, we are ready to learn the wonderful art of being still before God.

Chapter 5
Pre-Requisites: Solitude

The need for solitude and quietness was
never greater than it is today.

—A. W. Tozer

Before taking the first step toward
learning the art of waiting on **God,** it would be well
to consider motivation. Why do I want to learn
silent prayer? The correct answer would be: to come
closer to God, to love Him more, to live in His
presence, to serve Him more effectively.

Most of us, however, will include in motivation
more selfish yet legitimate reasons. We make the
humbling confession that although we have been
Christians for some years, instead of growing in
love for Jesus, we seem to have lost our "first love."
Instead of restfully and joyfully living in His
presence, we are often "burdened and heavy laden."

Then the realization of our lack impels us to
pray, "Dear God, if learning to be still before you
will help me find that 'place of quiet rest, near to
the heart of God,' then may I sit at your feet as did
Mary. I want to learn of you."

God will answer the prayer of those who long
for a more satisfying relationship with Jesus—who

want the rest which comes from truly knowing God and living in His presence.

God has many ways to answer a prayer like that. The most obvious and simple one is to enable us to respond to the invitation of Jesus:

> **Come unto me,** all *ye* that labour and
> are heavy laden, and I will give you rest.
> (Matt. 11:28)

We accept His invitation and COME TO HIM, asking Him to teach us to be still enough before Him so that He can give us His rest. The first lesson He will teach us is that we must take time to be ALONE WITH HIM.

And so we begin with QUIETNESS, SOLITUDE. Away from the wearisome chores and chatter and clatter of home and family: the crying of the baby, disputes of grade-schoolers, the raucous records of teens; away from the blare of television, even from singers on some Christian programs belting out gospel hymns to the jungle beat of rock music.

Away from the non-stop talker on the phone, from the neighbor who frequently drops in for coffee-klatch and endless recital of trivialities; away from the "maddening crowds" outside the home, where you can't even buy a loaf of bread without being assaulted by volumes of rock music at the super market.

Away from the cacophony of sounds at our places of employment; and finally away from the nervous rush of traffic as we turn again homeward.

Jesus told us that when we pray we are to enter the closet and shut the door upon the outside distractions and enclose ourselves with Him in SOLITUDE.

But people react differently to this suggestion. "Solitude! Who wants that? I can't stand it," cries the widow, the single woman, the divorced man. "Solitude? Oh, if only I could get away, it would save my sanity," sighs the young mother, the harassed business man, the college student sharing an apartment with three others.

Whether we dread solitude or welcome it, most of us realize that we can never completely escape from a certain sense of loneliness which is part of human nature.

What we are inside, what we feel and experience and think, all that constitutes the hidden man of the heart, is something we can only partially share with others. Even to the most understanding spouse or parent or child or friend or pastor, we can never fully expose our innermost depths. And so we stand alone, a solitary being in the swirling sea of life.

The only way this innate loneliness and aloneness could be truly relieved would be to have someone who really empathized with that secret inner man. This one would have to be so close as to be part of us—inside of us.

That is exactly what God has provided through Christ indwelling the believer, uniting him to God. Only then can there be complete understanding, full rapport, spirit with spirit.

Without that intimate fellowship, man will never be satisfied; he will always have that vague sense of loneliness, of standing apart from all human beings.

Paradoxically, the best way to relieve this loneliness is by solitude. Not the kind of solitude of being alone with ourselves, but of being alone with God.

Chapter 6
Place and Time

Someone has said that the basic prerequisites for communion with God are: A quiet place, a quiet time and a quiet heart.

A QUIET PLACE

Finding a time for daily devotions (in which we include a period of silence) may be simple or difficult, depending one one's circumstances. The working person who must pray in the early morning hours often has a problem finding privacy. It would be ideal if every home had a place reserved only for prayer and privacy. Since most homes do not, the closet of prayer will have to be discovered or improvised. For many it must be in the car or train, while riding to work.

The housewife can more easily find a place, often a comfortable chair in bedroom or living room. But wherever it is, it is a good idea to accustom yourself to some regular spot as your "sacred and hallowed retreat."

A.W. Tozer, one of the outstanding men of God of the 20th century, said,

> [1]Retire from the world each day to some private spot, even if it be only the

bedroom. (For a while I retreated to the furnace room for want of a better place.) Stay in the secret place till the surrounding noises begin to fade out of your heart, and a sense of God's presence envelopes you.

Deliberately tune out the unpleasant sounds and come out of your closet determined not to hear them. Listen for the inward Voice till you learn to recognize it. . . . Learn to pray inwardly every moment. After a while you can do this even while at work. . . . The discipline recommended will go far to neutralize the evil effects of externalism and make us acquainted with God and our own souls.

Even though you may have a place for a tryst with God, it will not necessarily be a quiet one. We can never exclude the unavoidable sounds of life around us. In the city or suburb we contend with barking dogs, shouts of preschool children, the roar of an airplane, occasionally the uplifting chime of church bells. To most of us these sounds have become so familiar that we no longer hear them.

Then there is always the phone, which some people shut off during prayer. (I have notified friends not to call during my time of devotions.) But we can't fully order our circumstances. The best way to get along with distracting sounds and noises is not to argue with them. If we accept them, they will be more apt to slide off with less interior friction.

Whenever possible, Christians should go out of doors for a time daily. The working person or busy mother will be able to be alone outside only at infrequent intervals. But there is nothing so refreshing to the spirit as a walk alone with God in a natural setting—a quiet park or woods, even a tree-lined street in a quiet residential area.

Of course God is not limited to revealing Himself or blessing us only in our appointed places of solitary retreat. I have been blessed by the Lord in the most unorthodox places.

One afternoon, while awaiting a train in a busy station, and being wedged between two large ladies who cast about me a screen of tobacco smoke, I turned my heart to Jesus. Soon I was engulfed in such a wonderful sense of His presence that I forgot my environment. The wearisome effects of shopping ebbed away and I returned home refreshed in the sweetness of the Lord.

Nevertheless, though God will meet us at any place, it is best to have a regular location for our daily tryst with God. After determining the place, we must next find a quiet time.

A QUIET TIME

For many, the time element is the biggest problem. First, as to when to pray, that is, the time of day—morning or evening or otherwise. Second, as to how long a period—fifteen minutes, half an hour, one hour.

If we are to give God our best, if we are to seek first the kingdom of God, then the logical time would be the first thing in the morning, when we are at our peak physically and mentally—refreshed and alert after a night's rest.

Obviously, if a man must be at work by seven AM, he might have to arise at 5:30 in order to have half an hour alone with God.

But if he regularly watches the late TV show, secular or Christian, and retires at midnight, he would not be likely to awaken early—feeling refreshed. Depending on how much sleep each person requires, adjustments will have to be made at the other end of the day, i. e. getting to bed earlier. It will require sacrifice, discipline, determination. Whether a person is willing to pay that price depends on his sense of values. Anything that is worthwhile costs.

The best way to prove the benefit of a regular time of devotions would be to try for a few months. If at the end of that time of "sacrifice" of the best time of our day to God, we do not find that we have grown spiritually, we can always try another approach.

The thousands of Christians who have given God the best part of their day attest to its being the very foundation of their Christian growth.

LENGTH OF TIME

Unless we take time, time enough with God for His light to shine into the depths of our hearts, it is vain for us to expect that His immeasurable love can enter our hearts and fill our lives.

—Author unknown.

Assuming that we have determined to take time for God in the morning, the next factor is to plan the length of time. (We must remember that whatever time we are able to give to devotions is not to be completely used for silent communion. It should include vocal prayer and Bible reading.)

Length of time will be determined by available time within circumstances—whether one is a working person, a mother of a young family or a retired person. When we sing "Sweet Hour of Prayer," we may be speaking figuratively. But those who actually do give an hour will most certainly benefit more greatly.

We must be honest about how much time we can spare. Often it is more than we think.

A housewife who feels she spends just a little time on her hobby of needle craft may be astonished at the end of the week to find it amounts to many hours. By comparison her devotions, which she believes consume an hour or so daily, by actual timing may be much shorter.

The work-weary husband may feel that he relaxes a mere half hour or so every evening before the TV or with the newspaper. By actual tabulation he may discover it to be one or two hours. At the same time he may lament that he has so little time for devotions. He really would find it much more relaxing, as well as spiritually refreshing, to spend fifteen minutes of that time just being still in the presence of God.

If we are serious about the development of our inner lives, we will pray with the Psalmist,

> So teach *us* to number our days that we
> may apply *our* hearts unto wisdom.
> (Psalm 90:12)

Chapter 7
How To Begin

I have done nothing but open windows—
God has done the rest.

—Frank Laubach

Suppose you take half an hour for devotions before going to your place of employment or before tending to household duties. You go to your "prayer closet" taking with you a Bible, a clock and a timing device—such as is used in the kitchen.

Before beginning devotions, offer a prayer to the Father in the name of Jesus, invoking the power of His name and of His blood and the aid of the Holy Spirit.

Proceed with regular devotions, that is, intercessory prayer and Bible reading. To begin, use passages on waiting on God (see list in back cf book), or look up passages in your concordance such as silence, rest, waiting, quiet.

This will prepare you for silent communion. If you plan on a half hour of devotions, you might want to allow five or ten minutes at the end for silence. Later you will arrange your own routine, allowing as much time for prayer, Bible and worship as you are led to. It is better to have a pattern, with the understanding that it will be flexible.

Since you have found a quiet place and a quiet time, you are now ready for a quiet heart.

A QUIET HEART

You are seated in a comfortable chair; (a prone position encourages slumber). Your body is still, you are not fidgeting; your voice is still, you are not engaged in oral prayer; your mind is still, you are not thinking about problems; you are not praying mentally. Now you are ready—not to empty your mind but to center it upon the Lord.

With a deep sigh, you relax, sinking into God like a babe into its mother's arms.

> [1]Lord I have given up my pride and turned away from my arrogance. I am not concerned with great matters or with subjects too difficult for me. Instead, I am content and at peace. As a child lies quietly in its mother's arms, so my heart is quiet within me.
> (Psalm 131:1-2 TEV)

> [2]Surely I have calmed and quieted my soul, like a weaned child with his mother; like a weaned child is my soul within me [ceased from fretting].
> (Psalm 131:2 TAB)

As an infant peacefully and trustfully looks up into its mother's face, so you are looking into the face of Jesus, setting your affections, your attention upon Him. (At this point you are not trying to "listen"—that will come later.) Just remain relaxed and still and attentive to Jesus.

While you attempt to center your mind on the Lord, you soon discover that you don't know exactly how to proceed. You find yourself praying, "Lord help me to concentrate on You. Help me to worship. Help me . . . ." And then you think, "But I'm not supposed to be praying; I'm supposed to be just loving Jesus."

"I really don't know how. I'll have to find out more about it. I wonder if I should read a book. What book . . . ? Oh, thinking of books, that reminds me, I have to order one for Jim's birthday. Then Aunt Mary's birthday is coming soon. I never know what to get her. Poor soul, she's getting so helpless . . . ."

Suddenly you realize that your mind has gone far astray. You glance at the clock; five minutes have elapsed. You really didn't have much silent communion. You sigh somewhat ruefully, wondering if you should repeat this attempt. Still, you notice that you do feel something—a touch of His peace and rest, a gentle sense of His sweetness and presence. Yes, it was worth while after all. This little time of quiet, or trying to be quiet, was truly blessed. And you think of the old song:

> [3]What a wonderful salvation
> Where we always see His face;
> What a perfect habitation,
> What a quiet resting place.
>
> Blessed quietness, holy quietness—
> What assurance in my soul.
> On the stormy sea

He speaks peace to me;
How the billows cease to roll!
                    — Manie P. Ferguson

And you conclude, "Yes I can see how wonderful it would be to always see His face." If only I could control those wandering thoughts, I believe this practice could develop into something beautiful.

Chapter 8
Wandering Thoughts

> Thou wilt keep him in perfect peace
> whose mind is stayed on Thee, because
> he trusteth in Thee.   (Isaiah 26:3)

This promise is attractive to the Christian seeking inner tranquility. However, the beginner in the practice of silent prayer will not have embarked upon his spiritual journey for very long before he realizes that the key words in this verse are "whose mind is stayed on Thee." And he has already discovered that this is not as easy as he thought.

His body may be still, his voice silent, but alas, his mind is a beehive of activity. When engaged in various duties—even when busy praying—the mind is occupied. But when trying to be still inwardly, the beginner realizes perhaps for the first time just how much "silent pandemonium" reigns within.

And now he understands the need for such a scripture as,

> "Wherefore gird up the loins of your
> mind, . . ."   (1 Peter 1:13-)

Although this state of perpetual mental and emotional agitation is especially characteristic of the twentieth century, it was by no means unknown to the slower-paced generations of the past. One reason why the monastic system arose and flourished was because even then many sought to get away from the "maddening crowd" of their own day. To their dismay, however, they discovered that in the silent deserts and monastery cells they still had to contend with and conquer the incessant interior turmoil.

Lest we be tempted to lose interest in learning silent communion, let's be encouraged by the accomplishment of A. B. Simpson who wrote:

> [1]A score of years ago a friend placed in my hand a little book which became one of the turning points in my life. It was *TRUE PEACE* . . . an old medieval message which had but one thought—
>
> *God is waiting in the depth of my being to talk with me, if I would only get still enough to hear him.*
>
> So I began to get still.
>
> But I had no sooner commenced than a perfect pandemonium of voices reached my ears, a thousand clamoring notes from without and within, until I could hear nothing but their noise and din. Some of them were my own questions, some of them my own cares, some of them my own prayers. Others were the suggestions of the Tempter and the voices of the world's turmoil. Never

before did there seem so many things to be done, to be said, to be thought; and in every direction I was pulled and pushed and greeted with noisy acclamations and unspeakable unrest.

It seemed necessary for me to listen to some of them, but God said, 'Be still and know that I am God.' Then came the conflict of thoughts for the morrow and its duties and cares; but God said, "Be Still."

As I slowly learned to obey and shut my ears to every sound, I found that after a while when the other voices ceased or I ceased to hear them, there was a still,small voice in the depth of my spirit.

As I listened, it became to me the power of prayer, the voice of wisdom and the call of duty. And I did not need to think so hard or pray so hard or trust so hard. That still, small voice of the Holy Spirit in my heart was God's answer to all my questions.

Eventually every person who seriously works at staying his mind on God will experience a wonderful sense of His presence. This will bring not only his spirit into rest, but his body and mind as well.

But it will take time.

Chapter 9

Starting All Over Again

> Truly my soul waiteth upon God [King
> James Version margin: *is silent to God*]:
> from him *cometh* my salvation.
>
> (Psalm 62:1)

Now that we understand that learning to be still is not quite as simple as we had at first believed, it might be a good idea to start all over again.

No longer are we standing up cocksure. We are where we belong, at the feet of Jesus. We do not now feel that "presto, chango," we will become top-notch saints in a few weeks, but we are prepared to spend a little time working to gain so great a prize.

So now we are again seated in a relaxed position, eyes closed and body and voice still. We try to turn our attention to God. But here they come trooping in—thoughts of every kind. What shall we do now?

In this chapter I will list several methods to help stay the mind, one of which is:

1. USING A DEVOTIONAL BOOK

The minister who was my teacher suggested that I begin by putting my attention on Jesus in love and worship. When my mind began to wander, he told me to read a little in *WAITING ON GOD,* by Andrew Murray. Here is a portion of a sample paragraph:

> [1] . . . bow quietly before God, just to remember and realize who he is, how near he is, how certainly he can and will help. Just be still before him and allow his Holy Spirit to waken and stir up in your soul the childlike disposition of absolute dependence and confident expectation. Wait upon God as a Living Being, as the Living God who notices you and is longing to fill you with his salvation. . . . Wait on God till you know you have met Him. . . .

After having read a few sentences, which have met their purpose of turning the wandering mind again to God, then close your eyes and remain attentive to Him.

When, shortly, you find yourself thinking about the letter you must write or that dental appointment—read again until you are centered on God. Then commune silently, lovingly.

This is the method I used for many months. At first it will seem that the entire period allotted to communion is spent in just *trying.* This is the normal reaction. This is the path every lover of Jesus followed, and it is the one you will have to take.

It does require discipline and persistence. But you will discover, even at the end of a few weeks, that you are already beginning to learn *how to con-*

centrate on God. And you begin to feel the sweetness and tranquility of His presence—even if only briefly.

2. SCRIPTURE

An excellent way to stay the mind is with Scripture. You might wonder why I didn't begin that way, instead of with a book. It is because reading a book, especially one which instructs on silent prayer like, *WAITING ON GOD*, by Andrew Murray, or, *Practice Of The Presence Of God*, by Brother Lawrence, is an easier way to begin.

In silent worship your aim is to "behold the Lord." You center your spirit on the Lord Himself, in order to experience this Jesus of whom the Scriptures write.

When you use Scripture to help you stay your mind, it would be well to select, for your worship, verses which describe some attribute of the Lord. In this way your mind will be directed to the Lord Himself, and He becomes the Living Word. You might also want to use some of the Scriptures listed in the back of this book.

3. THE LORD'S PRAYER

Another way to use Scripture is with the Lord's prayer. Begin with "our Father;" contemplate on the meaning of those words until you are brought into His presence. If your mind goes off in another direction (as it most surely will), think again of those words, or softly murmur "my Father." Do this repeatedly until your mind remains fixed upon the

Lord. The next day use the following phrase, "which art in heaven."

4. THE JESUS PRAYER

A still more simple and direct means to stay the mind is by a single word: Jesus. Every time your mind wanders, repeat that name inside, until your attention is again drawn back to God.

5. OTHER WAYS

Personally, I often use the name of Jesus or of the Father or of the Holy Spirit. One cannot be rigid about any of these means. Sometimes if a song is in my mind, I let the phrases or words sing within, helping me to center on Jesus. At times I mentally repeat a phrase like "Jesus, you are within," or "Jesus, I am turning my heart to you."

Just so your mind doesn't become too active as you use these devices. As you practice, you will be led by the Spirit into what means to use at what times. It is best not to engage in a direct contest with distracting thoughts, but simply turn away from them by looking inward and paying attention to Jesus.

Your determination to center upon the Lord involves, of course, an act of your will. Scripture supports such action:

> Set your affection on things above, . . .
> (Col. 3:3-)
> . . . study to be quiet, . . . (1 Thes. 4:-11-)

> My heart is fixed, O God, . . .
> (Psalm 57:7-)

But it must be done gently, peacefully, as Laubach says:

> [2]This simple practice requires only a gentle pressure of the will, not more than a person can exert easily. It grows easier as the habit becomes fixed. Yet it transforms life into heaven.

As we persevere in continually returning our thoughts inward, we will gradually be able to remain silent in His presence more easily and for longer periods.

Every person who has persevered until he has learned how to stay his mind on the Lord will agree that he has come into closer relationship with Him.

These are the beginning results of silent communion. More will be said later about deeper forms. Not everyone, perhaps only a few, will have the inclination or will take the time to engage in these deeper forms.

As a matter of fact, not everyone will be interested in any kind of silent communion, simple or advanced. Some are *Marthas* by nature, others are *Marys*, who by temperament find it easier to be contemplative.

But all, including busy *Marthas*, will receive the blessing of even the simplest forms of communion if they will at least now and then take "a time to be silent."

BIBLE REFERENCES FOR
Chapter 10, Page 49 (next)

Know ye not that ye are the temple of God, and *that* the Spirit of God dwelleth in you? If any man defile the temple of God, him shall God destroy; for the temple of God is holy, which *temple* ye are.

(1 Corinthians 3:16-17)

What? know ye not that your body is the temple of the Holy Ghost *which is* in you, which ye have of God, and ye are not your own? For ye are bought with a price: therefore glorify God in your body, and in your spirit, which are God's.   (1 Corinthians 6:19-20)

And what agreement hath the temple of God with idols? for ye are the temple of the living God; as God hath said, I will dwell in them, and walk in *them*; and I will be their God, and they shall be my people.

(2 Corinthians 6:16)

Chapter 10
The Silence Break

Let's assume that by now you have added, to your regular time of devotions, a period of being still before the Lord. You have found it a blessed practice and have decided to continue doing so. However, as delightful and beneficial as is the practice of regular times of being still before God, there is additional blessing for those who learn to take "silence breaks" at various times of the day.

Employees are usually granted a fifteen minute coffee break in the middle of the morning and of the afternoon. Studies have proved these intervals of rest promote efficiency. This practice is fine. But I am suggesting something much better for a Christian: *Take a silence break instead.*

It would be wonderful to have a little retreat where we could be alone with God. Obviously we cannot carry a hideout wherever we go. But here is good news—the Bible says that if we have received Christ, then our bodies are the house, the temple, the dwelling place of God.

(Ref. 1 Cor. 3:16-17; 6:19-20; 2 Cor. 6:16 — See opposite Pg.)

So we actually do carry a hideout wherever we go! We can turn within and commune with God any time of the day or night and in any place—home, office, shop, car, bus, social gatherings and even in church!

Let's look into various ways to take this silence break.

Here is Jane, a housewife. Early in the morning she had her half hour of devotions, concluding with a ten minute time of being still. She felt calm and close to God afterward. But by the time she had finished her weekly grocery shopping, nearly had an accident with the car, unloaded groceries—whatever uplift she had received from her morning communion had already dissipated into the stream of rushing traffic on the highway going home.

While she sat at the table sipping coffee, she remembered the silence break. Closing her eyes, she sighed deeply and relaxed into her chair, turning her mind and heart to Jesus. For a moment she felt Him draw close.

Then she was distracted by the sound of a car outside and her mind went back to her near accident. Then to the crowded highway and then to their need of a new car and then—**suddenly** she remembered she was to be waiting on God and again turned her mind to Jesus.

Into her heart there drifted a line of a song she had heard on her car radio: "How Sweet the Name of Jesus Sounds." She let the melody flow through her mind, into her heart. She murmured that name. How lovely He was! He had drawn near again, or was it that she had drawn near and that He had been there, waiting for her attention?

When the click of the refrigerator distracted her, she opened her eyes and glanced at the clock. Ten minutes had elapsed—blessed, God-filled minutes. So this was her "silence break!" Wonderful! She would try it again.

As she arose to her day's duties, the aura of His presence remained with her for some time.

After the children returned from school, gulped down snacks and ran off into different directions, Jane began thinking of the evening meal. But she was weary again and needed another "silence break." This time she didn't bother with coffee but just sank into the easy chair and took another *mini silence break*. When she arose at the sound of the dog barking for attention, she was enveloped in the presence of God.

Her husband John had his half hour of devotions before breakfast. During the half hour drive to work he tried to maintain the presence of the Lord. At intersections when the light was red, he turned his heart to the Lord. And he felt that certain warmth and glow of the approaching Presence.

After a few busy hours at the office, he joined the 10:30 trek to the coffee urn. Minutes later, he returned to his desk, turning his heart to God, taking a *silence break*. Refreshed, he was ready for work again.

The hypothetical man and wife represent idealized experiences. It isn't always that easy and rewarding. Yet if this couple keeps working at learning to be still at home and during the workday, the ideal will be realized in varying degrees.

It doesn't just happen, however; we have to be informed of the possibility of living like this. We must also be convinced that it will work and will make a great difference in life. Therefore, we will have to deliberately plan the times when we can and should take *mini silence breaks.* Life isn't always so serene and peaceful and orderly, but we can do a few things to make it more so.

PLANNING THE SILENCE BREAKS

Before going to any destination, we may keep busy to the last minute, then dash into the car still buttoning our coats, arriving barely on time. Or we can allow five extra minutes for a Quiet time by arriving at our destination a little early.

For a dental appointment, for instance, why not arrive five minutes early? Be seated, take a magazine and under pretext of reading, commune with God. You will not be nearly so tense by the time you sit in *the chair!*

While awaiting a bus or train or while parked before a long freight, instead of fuming or passing time in trivial talk, why not use those precious moments for communing with God?

Even at social gatherings, when the room is buzzing with small talk, why not take a seat in a corner for a while and though appearing to listen, just allow your heart to turn to Jesus for a few moments. It will bless your own soul and will change the atmosphere around you. You might be surprised to find the empty chatter turning into conversation about God.

When preparing to go to church, plan to arrive at least five minutes early,so you can sit quietly in the sanctuary, looking to Jesus. It will help increase His presence in the meeting.

Even during the church service you can wait on God. Some meetings are so busy from beginning to end that somehow you haven't been able to really contact the Lord. Why not let your heart turn to Jesus in a few moments of inner communion (not during the preaching, unless it is exceedingly dull)—perhaps during a solo. After all, you came to meet God, not to go through religious exercises.

What a difference this practice of communing with God during the moments will make. How it will bring calm to the soul and rest to the body. How it will ease the pangs of loneliness, lift the cloud of depression. How it will raise you into the presence of God and center your life around Himself. Things of the material world will increasingly recede and you will find yourself more and more occupied with the Lord and with His kingdom.

Mrs. Martha Robinson, a saintly woman who lived in the early 20th century, said:

> [1]Whenever you can, take a few minutes of just waiting on Jesus, not necessarily praying, but just waiting, looking into His face, desiring His presence.
>
> At first you may not seem to receive much, but if you take every opportunity, presently your soul will hunger for Him. The sweetness of Himself will come to you and you will become like lovers. You

would rather slip away with Him for a minute or two than to talk or read or rest or eat. And when you are tired or rushed or nervous, a few minutes with Him in the stillness of His presence will rest you more than anything in the world.

What happens as a result? Mrs. Robinson said:

The soul is transformed. We are changed and brought into great peace. We are immunized to conditions, people and life itself—all the things that would turn us from the fullness of His love, peace and rest.

Andrew Murray in *Waiting On God* wrote:

[2]Though at first it may appear difficult to know how thus quietly to wait, with the activities of mind and heart for a time subdued, every effort at it will be rewarded; we shall find that it grows upon us and the little season of silent worship will bring a peace and rest that give a blessing not only in prayer, but all the day.

Taking brief moments to be still is a wonderful addition to the spiritual life. However this should not replace regular times of waiting on God in definite, appointed places and times. It is only during these more extended periods of devotions, that the Lord can begin to really bring us into deeper blessings of silent communion.

Chapter 11
Talkativeness

... let thy words be few.   (Ecc. 5:-2)

The interior life consists in very few
words and a great tendency to God.
                    —Mother Marguerite

Really, nothing more than the above need be
said about the relation between talkativeness and
inwardness.

The first requirements for waiting on God are
to still the voice, the body, the mind. During devotions this may be comparatively easy. But if we are
to carry our communion with God beyond the
prayer room and into the stream of life, it will not
be so simple to be sparing in our words.

The Bible has something to say about quietness
in daily life:
We are told to study to be quiet,   (Ref. 1 Thess. 4:11)
To work with quietness,   (Ref. 2 Thess. 3:12)
To live a quiet and peaceable life,   (Ref. 1 Tim. 2:2)
Women are urged to have a meek and quiet spirit.
                              (Ref. 1 Peter 3:4)

If we want to discover how seldom these sug-
gestions are followed, we could try being an

observer instead of a participant in the following situations:

Listen to the chatter at the dinner table or when a friend drops in. At your place of work, during coffee break, you will be amazed at how many words people take to say exactly nothing. At social gatherings the unbelievable amount of empty words will surprise you.

As for some telephone conversations . . . !

To top it all: Listen to the volumes of empty, pre-meeting chatter. Subjects vary from split pea soup to the big fish that got away. Some talkers continue at intervals during the entire service.

How much better to lift our hearts to God for a moment—at the dinner table, in social gatherings, at work and above all, while awaiting the church service to begin.

I am not saying we should never communicate but it would be well to do so within the context of the advice given in Proverbs 17:27-:

> He that hath knowledge spareth his
> words: . . .

The person who aspires to walk with God will hardly have to be told to limit his words. Something of a holy hush comes upon one during the first moments after having been in communion with God. If we add to our day frequent moments of silences it would help control the flow of (often empty) words which would normally pour out of us.

I know of no better way to conclude this chapter than by quoting an entire tract, whose author is unknown, but whose words have helped many who are seeking to walk in the inward way:

¹TALKATIVENESS

Talkativeness is utterly ruinous to deep spirituality. It is one of the greatest hindrances to deep, solid union with God. Notice how people will tell the same thing over and over—how insignificant trifles are magnified by a world of words; how things that should be buried are dragged out into gossip and disputed over; how the solemn, deep things of the Holy Spirit are rattled over in a light manner—until one who has the real baptism of divine silence in his heart feels he must unceremoniously tear himself away to some lonely room or forest where he can gather up the fragments of his mind and rest in God.

Not only do we need cleansing from sin, but our natural human spirit needs a radical death to its own noise and activity and wordiness.

See the evil effects of so much talk.

First: It dissipates the spiritual power. The thought and feeling of the soul are like powder and steam—the more they are condensed, the greater their power.

Second: It is a waste of time. If the hours spent in useless conversation were spent in prayer or reading, we would soon reach a region of soul life and divine peace beyond our present dreams.

Third: Loquacity inevitably leads to saying unwise or unpleasant or unprofitable things. In religious conversation we soon churn up all the cream our souls have in them and the rest of our talk is all pale skim milk, until we get alone with God and feed on His green pastures until the cream rises again.

The Holy Spirit warns us that "In the multitude of words there wanteth not sin: . . . ." It is impossible for even the best of saints to talk beyond a certain point without saying something unkind or severe or foolish or erroneous.

(Ref. Proverbs 10:19-)

We must settle this personally. If others are noisy and gossip, I must determine to live in constant quietness and humility of heart. I must guard my speech as a sentinel does a fortress. With all respect for others, I must many times cease from conversation or withdraw from company to enter into communion with my precious Lord.

To walk in the Spirit we must avoid talking for talk's sake or merely to entertain. To speak effectively we must speak in God's appointed time and in harmony with the indwelling Holy Spirit.

Chapter 12
Various Aspects of Stillness

When we begin to be still before the Lord we are encouraged and attracted by its initial results—the lovely sense of His presence, the tranquility of body and soul, a deeper love for Jesus Himself. But as we continue, we discover that its highest benefits are not cheaply obtained.

Matthew 5:8 says:

> Blessed are the pure in heart for they shall see God.

If we want to make any real progress in communion with God one of the prices to pay will be cooperation with the Holy Spirit in His efforts to bring us into some degree of purity of heart.

PURITY OF HEART

The nearer we draw to God, the more we become aware of the impurities which cause us to:

> . . . see through a glass darkly; . . .
> (1 Cor. 13:-12-)

As we submit to the purging process we will find veil after veil being stripped away and the face of Jesus becoming more and more clearly visible. Nothing is so devastating to sin and self as the work of the Holy Spirit when we are engaged in silent communion.

Eventually we will so cherish God's presence that we will be careful . . . .

> . . . to have always a conscience void of offence toward God, and *toward* men.
> (Acts 24:-16)

Personally, I have found that even lesser infractions of the laws of God, such as speaking sharply or unkindly, raise a barrier between God and myself. I cannot approach Him with confidence until I make things right. Often He rewards me out of proportion to my repentance.

This happened one day when the Lord showed me that for months I had been harboring resentments against a mechanic who overcharged me for car repairs. At the urging of the Holy Spirit I submitted to the embarrassment of asking the man for forgiveness, explaining that I could not bear to hold a grudge against anyone. He gruffly accepted my apology. (Incidentally, he didn't charge me for the present minor repair! And we've been good friends ever since. He even calls me "Dolly!")

During my devotions the next day, the Lord poured over my soul unusual glory. To me it was His way of indicating pleasure at the action of the previous day. I have frequently found that when I humble myself in order to have some measure of purity of heart, I am rewarded by being able too "see God" more clearly.

Much more could be said about the relation between purity of heart and our ability to see God. When I began to realize some of the requirements for successful communion with God, I was at first somewhat less than eager to pursue my course.

As I continued trudging the sometimes arduous path to the promised land, I was encouraged enough by some of its delights to even feel willing to engage in combat with any giant I might encounter. I discovered there were several.

RELUCTANCE

Generally speaking, I look forward to daily devotions. But for some reason, when it is time to be still before the Lord, I am sometimes reluctant to begin. It must be that lazy streak which wants to avoid the effort it takes to regulate the mind.

> . . . the spirit indeed *is* willing, but the flesh *is* weak.   (Matt. 26:-41)

Nevertheless, I usually do conclude my devotions with a period of silence.

But I have not yet disposed of Giant Reluctance, for he exerts his influence during the day when I make attempts to have several "silence breaks." My problem is: I get so involved with manifold duties that when the Lord gently suggests that I be still for a while, both in body as well as soul, I feel indisposed to interrupt the continuity of my pace, even though I know from many past, experiences how helpful it will be.

This form of self-will is implied in the latter part of this passage:

> For thus saith the Lord GOD, the Holy
> One of Israel; In returning and rest shall
> ye be saved; in quietness and confidence
> shall be your strength: and ye would not.
> But ye said, No; for we will flee upon
> horses; . . .   (Isa. 30:15-16-)

So I am constantly having to discipline myself to get off those swift horses and to rest in the Lord. Not always but usually, I simply stop what I am doing, sink into a chair, close my eyes and wait on the Lord. Though it often seems just a time of **trying**, yet I am always glad I did—glad enough even to be willing to tackle any other giant in the way.

Sure enough, here he comes! But who is this creature, so limp and languid that I scarce consider him worth my attention? His name is Inertia.

INERTIA

This is a giant who especially troubles new-comers learning the prayer of silence.

Some days I may feel tired or ill or whatever. I seem able to more or less acceptably complete regular devotions. Then I begin communing in silence, as I think. A plane roaring overhead awakens me. Awakens? Yes, to my chagrin I discover my head is sunken upon my chest, or worse, I may have snored a loud, slurpy snore. I had spent the entire time in slumber instead of waiting on God!

To overcome Giant Inertia, simple and effective weapons are available. Get up and walk around a little. Praise God audibly. Sing. Read from a devotional book.

We are told, in Hebrews 6:12:

> That ye be not slothful but followers of them who through faith and patience inherit the promises.

Since we are acquiring a habit which will be so invaluable, we can expect Satan to be lurking nearby. Without fanfare, we should resist him by the above means and also by quietly and firmly invoking the name of Jesus and the power of His blood. It is interesting to observe that James 4:-7 which says:

> . . . Resist the devil and he will flee from you.

is followed by:

> Draw nigh to God and He will draw nigh to you. . . .   (James 4:8-)

As we refuse to yield to Giant Inertia and press on toward God, the Lord will reward us with greater manifestations of His presence.

Chapter 13
Listening

. . . Speak, Lord; for thy servant heareth.
. . .   (1 Sam. 3:-9-)

[1]Lord, I have shut the door, speak now
the word, Which in the din and throng,
could not be heard. Hushed now my
inner heart, whisper thy will While I
have come apart, while all is still.

—William M. Runyan

To some, communion means *listening
to God*. I have not previously mentioned this aspect
for particular reasons. Unless and until one has advanced somewhat in this form of prayer and
acquired some degree of spiritual maturity, one
ought be cautious about being still before God with
the specific intent of doing so **in order to** hear from
God.

Because we are "frail children of dust," it is too
easy for an imaginative person to "hear God
speak"—which would often be in accord with personal desire.

Being sure one is hearing the Lord's voice and
not his own is a problem which has always troubled
Christians, particularly when seeking guidance.

Many excellent books have been written about guidance. Learning by one's own experience is also important.

Personally, I check on myself and profit by my own mistakes or successes. If I thought I had heard from the Lord and later discover it was my own idea, I come down a few pegs and resolve to be more careful next time. If I did truly hear from the Lord—and this is very often the case—and later events prove it to indeed be His voice, then I rejoice and give God thanks.

As we grow in our ability to be still it will also include an increased ability to rightly discern what comes to us as we "listen" to the Lord.

However, in subtle ways the listening **motive** during times of silence may take one off-center, conditioning him to be more concerned about hearing from God than about loving Him and simply being in His presence.

Having issued these generalized warnings, I affirm that God does speak to His people on rare occasions audibly but usually by the inner voice within the soul.

This is abundantly supported by Scripture. Isaiah promised:

> And thine ears shall hear a word behind thee, saying, This *is* the way, walk ye in it, when ye turn to the right hand, and when ye turn to the left.   (Isa. 30:21)

In John 10:4 Jesus tells us that His sheep know His voice. And James 1:5 assures us that if we lack wisdom we are to ask of God, who gives to all liberally.

Such personal guidance can become very much a part of daily life, as was discovered by Karen Mains who obviously is a mature Christian.

Quoting from her book, *Open Heart, Open Home:*

> [2]Prayer is a neglected Christian discipline, but the prayer of listening is the most neglected. We are familiar with requests, less comfortable with thanksgiving, intercessions, praise, confession, forgiveness; but we know next to nothing about sitting before the Lord in quietness, waiting upon Him.
>
> Each week, in addition to those other regular periods of prayer, I set aside several contemplation sessions. These may last from fifteen minutes to an hour. Beginning always with praise, once I am aware of being in the Presence of the Lord, I start the process of disciplining my mind to listen.
>
> It is indeed a discipline. All the human realities begin to interject themselves. Dinners need to be prepared, phone calls made, writing planned—No! It is You, Lord, I seek to hear, not these. Help me to fasten my mind on Your Presence.
>
> For many years I was tutored daily at His hand during sessions. It was amazing how much there was to learn. After a while I began to experience silence.

Sometimes there were infrequent directives as to ministry and fewer awesome reminders from the Word as to needs for inner correction. But I began to learn that the silence was in itself the voice of God. This is the quiet of the Spirit, a communication which occurs without words.

From the beginning of man's association with God, multitudes have been hearing God speak in every area of human need: guidance, comfort, spiritual insight, correction, practical information. Recently I received a letter from a woman who heard me speak about waiting on God at a retreat. She wrote:

[3]Last Tuesday was a personal crisis in my life and I needed some definite direction from the Lord. I took the day off and a friend and I met with the Lord. I understand now what you meant when you said that once you were lost in the presence of God for half an hour. That is exactly what happened. The Spirit of God just filled the apartment and held us in the most blessed peace and quietness that I've ever experienced.

In that quietness the Lord spoke to my spirit and told me that He was not allowing this trial except that it had a real purpose in my life and that I would come forth as gold. He also said that man would not lift me up—but that "I will lift you up." Of course I was greatly blessed.

The following day I saw the super-
natural power of God overrule a
circumstance that no man could have
changed. We serve a great God!

These "directives" from the Lord, of whatsoever
sort they may be, and on matters great or small, do
not necessarily come only during prayer or silence.
Often we hear God speak in the midst of our
workaday lives.

However, we are more likely to hear that inner
voice of God as we are quietly sitting at the feet of
Jesus with our minds stayed on Him.

Chapter 14
Beginning to Grow

BEGINNING TO GROW IN SILENT COMMUNION

That he would grant you, according to
the riches of his glory, to be
strengthened with might by his Spirit in
the inner man;   (Eph. 3:16)

[1]Each time you come to wait upon him or
to seek to maintain in daily life the holy
habit of waiting, you may look up and
see him ready to meet you, waiting that
he may be gracious unto you.
—Andrew Murray's *Waiting On God*

Suppose you have now been learning to be still
for six months. You have become careful about the
holiness part of your spiritual life. Although you
have frequently grappled with the giants: Wandering
Thoughts, Reluctance and Inertia, you don't feel
you have exactly driven them out of the promised
land, but at least you have "put them to tribute."

(Ref. Joshua 17:13)

Sometimes you do wonder how successful each
period of silence really is, because it seems such a
battle to try to stay your mind upon the Lord.

However, you are encouraged to learn from those who have perfected this art that we need not be overly concerned about imaginations or wandering thoughts, since they are really only on the surface of your being. Despite the annoyance of thoughts—the inner man, the spiritual man, has been truly communing with God. Therefore you have been making much more progress than you realized or understood.

The reason you agree that this must be true is that after several seemingly not very successful months at working to commune in silence, you do perceive gradual inner changes. You are closer to God, more aware of His presence and you respond to Him with greater warmth.

[2]Bernard of Clairvaux expresses your feelings at this point:

> We taste thee, O thou living bread,
> And long to feast upon thee still;
> We drink of thee, thou fountainhead
> And thirst our souls from thee to fill.

You also understand a little of what Frank Laubach said, which at first seemed extravagant:

> [3]We develop what Thomas A Kempis calls "a familiar friendship with Jesus." Our unseen friend becomes dearer, closer and more wonderful every day until at last we know him as "Jesus, lover of my soul," not only in song but in blissful experience. . . . This warm, ardent friendship ripens rapidly; and it keeps on growing richer and more radiant every month.

Now you begin to feel that it is lovely to be still before God, to sit at His feet. Of course, you are not on the mountain top every day. But you have beautiful moments often enough now so that you cherish your times of stillness, hoping that this day will be one of those when His presence becomes almost tangible—when he floods you with His love and you are able to carry the glow and glory of his presence into your day.

You also feel you are beginning to experience again "the first love," which is the awakening of the soul to the wonder of Jesus Himself. And you want to build three tabernacles, or at least one and just stay there, reveling in His presence.   (Ref. Rev. 2:4)

Should you become concerned that you are getting to be a spiritual glutton living for the enjoyment of the presence of God, be of good cheer. There is a remedy.

SPIRITUAL DRYNESS

Nearly everyone who has ever practiced silent prayer has experienced times when God seems nowhere around. This happens even to those who,like Brother Lawrence, habitually live in the presence of God. Some call the absence of spiritual consolations the "dark night of the soul," others designate it as the walk by pure faith alone.

This darkness may last a few days or weeks or months or, in rare cases, for years. At such times the Scriptures play a vital part in stabilizing the Christian and maintaining his determination to seek God regardless of the withdrawal of overt expressions of His love.

It would be difficult to pinpoint any single cause for this "dark night of the soul." It may be occasioned by sin, carelessness, neglect of prayer and Bible reading; it may result from prolonged illness or a severe test. Or God may simply permit it to happen in the ordinary course of life in order to try us.

It is comparatively easy to spend time with God when we are being caressed by His love. But are we then following Him because of His gifts and blessings? Or do we love Himself alone, whether or not we feel His presence? Are we willing to prove this when He seems to withdraw His presence and permits us to walk by faith?

This testing time could be compared to a wife faithfully visiting her husband who is in a coma. Daily she comes to the hospital, sits beside him for an hour, strokes his hand, lets her love go out to him, silently praying. She does this day after day, even though she receives absolutely no response.

To the person going through the valley of spiritual dryness, there always comes a day when he has passed through and emerges again into the brightness of His presence and glory. Each time this cycle occurs the relationship has deepened and we are more united than ever. And we can be trusted with more advanced forms of silent communion.

Chapter 15
More On Growth

[1]God is always awaiting the chance to give us high days. We so seldom are in deep earnest about giving Him the chance. —Laubach

TIMES OF UNUSUAL PRESENCE

Much of our communion will be on the natural basis, that is, we set our wills to be still before God. We make the necessary efforts to regulate our thoughts and overcome hindrances. We pray for the help of the Holy spirit.

But everyone who has ever waited on God for any length of time has experienced moments of an unusual presence of God.

This is when God, either suddenly or gradually comes to us so greatly that we can do nothing but remain in awed silence of soul and often stillness of body.

This happened to me one evening while I was in silent communion. Gradually I became completely immersed in a heavenly atmosphere. I became aware of only one thing—that God was very present and that presence was LOVE, an overwhelming, all encompassing love, surrounding me, within me, filling the room. It was absolutely marvellous.

For half an hour my entire being—mind, soul, spirit and body were transfixed. I don't know how long I would have remained in that tremendous awareness of God, but the phone shattered the glory of that moment.

I have had many lesser experiences like this, in which I did not even need to try to control my thoughts or set them on God, for the Lord Himself did that for me. I wouldn't even say that at such times I was consciously thinking of God, but that I was aware of Him in hushed, almost breathless awe.

Should we say that these times of unusual blessing come only to those who are advanced? No, I would not say so. Times of great awareness of God's presence often happen in meetings or during personal prayer—but especially so while being still before God. Beginners are often so blessed. But those who learn how to yield themselves wholly to God in stillness do experience many more of these high moments.

LENGTH OF TIME

When we are beginners a question arises. Let's say you have been trying for three months to learn how to be still. Though you are experiencing some of the wonderful fruits of this practice—increased sense of His presence, more joy and tranquility, more release from depression and loneliness—you are far from satisfied. And you wonder, "How long will it take, anyway?"

In my own experience, many changes took place after six months of learning to be still, about one hour daily. Obviously, if you spend only five or ten minutes, it will take longer—months or even a year or more. Perhaps it depends on how earnest we are about meeting God in this way; how much we value His presence.

To acquire skill in any endeavor—typing, piano, handicraft—includes drudgery, effort, diligence, practice for months. But even while learning, you are encouraged to go on because of the delights of beginning results. You can play a little tune or type a sentence or construct a simple bench.

God knows our particular situations. The mother of small children, the working person, the provider of the family have at their disposal much less time for devotions than a mother with grown children or a retired or a single person.

God does not expect of us the impossible. Neither, however, will He permit us to hide under the excuse of "no time," unless it is really true. We cannot plead lack of time to wait on God if we spend three hours daily watching TV (even Christian TV), reading the newspaper, books and magazines (even spiritual ones), spend too much time on the phone, fuss unnecessarily with the house or hobbies or whatnot.

Some things will have to be sacrificed. Anyone who has ever achieved success in any line had to sacrifice the good for the better and the better for the best. The athletes or musicians give up many legitimate pleasures and comforts. We can always find time to do what we really want to do. We can arrange our priorities—if we will.

But even if we are unwilling or unable to make sacrifices in order to really find God, whatever time we do give to prayer and silence will be rewarded proportionately. And often in His love and mercy God rewards us out of proportion to our efforts.

[2]Andrew Murray said in *Waiting On God:*

> The whole duty and blessedness of waiting on God has its root in this, that He is a Blessed Being, full to overflowing with goodness and power and life and joy. Therefore no one, however wretched, can for any time come into contact with Him without that life and power secretly, silently beginning to enter into him and blessing him.
>
> God is love. That is the only and all-sufficient warrant of our expectation, Love seeketh out its own. God's love is just His delight to impart Himself and His blessedness to His children. Come, and however feeble you feel, just wait in His presence.

RECEIVING

The reason God can make such a generous offer to even half-hearted seeking after Himself, is because it is His nature to bestow Himself.

I have said that this book will stress silent communion, in which we are not seeking anything for ourselves or others but are ministering to God, giving to Him.

Nevertheless, it would be contrary to the nature of God for Him to be only **receiving**. It is His nature to give: good gifts to those who ask, help and comfort, healing and guidance—all we need. He seeks only our highest and best welfare.

That is why He longs to bestow His best gift, which is Himself. He knows that though we might be sick or poor or forsaken or lonely, with Him, we can be at peace.

Many Christians, particularly women, are depressed and lonely for various reasons: divorce, widowhood, spinsterhood—with little possibility of change in their status on the human level. But on the divine level their needs can be met. Countless Christians over the centuries have discovered that having been denied or lost human consolations, they found that their need to love and be loved was met by the love of Jesus.

But this love must be nourished and the best way is by often sitting at the feet of Jesus, looking into His face. However, God can give only in proportion to our capacity to receive. So it is encouraging to know that one of the blessings of silent communion is that as we spend time with Him, He enlarges our capacity to respond to Him and to contain more and more of Himself.

When we first met the Lord, many of our spiritual blessings were "soulish" and on a superficial level. But as we grow in God and our capacity is enlarged, during the time of silent communion we learn to meet Him on a much deeper and more satisfying level—spirit with Spirit. It is here that deep inner changes take place.

Chapter 16
Results of Being Still

The fellowship of God is delightful
beyond all telling.
                      —A. W. Tozer

After you have practiced silence for six months or more you will notice certain changes taking place in spirit, soul and even body.

1. GREATER AWARENESS OF GOD'S PRESENCE

First you will find that as you have drawn near to God, He has indeed drawn near to you. Of course, He is always present, but now we become more aware of it.

Your soul will be much more responsive to Jesus. As you develop in this, you will be able to commune with God in locations other than your place of prayer—in the supermarket checkout line, railroad station, in your car.

2. JOY

You will soon discover that His presence always brings joy. Most often it is the quiet joy of Psalm 104:34:

My meditation of Him shall be sweet:
I will be glad in the Lord.

At times you will experience greater degrees of happiness:

> . . . in thy presence *is* fulness of joy; . . .
>
> (Psalm 16:11)

Out of her own experience Fanny Crosby wrote:

> [1]Oh the pure delight of a single hour
> That before thy throne I spend;
> When I kneel in prayer and with thee,
> my God,
> I commune as friend with Friend.

If you fear being self-centered in your enjoyment of God, read John 15:11 where Jesus tells us that He desires His joy to remain in us and our joy to be full.

Communion gladdens God's heart as well. Proverbs 8:-31 says:

> . . . my delights *were* with the sons of men.

And Zepheniah 3:17 says:

> The Lord thy God . . . will joy over thee with singing.

If God takes such delight in the sons of men, should we deprive Him of this joy?

3. TRANQUILITY

> Thou wilt keep *him* in perfect peace *whose* mind *is* stayed *on thee:* . . .
>
> (Isa. 26:3-)

Early in silent communion you will experience a new sense of peace and rest.

William Runyan wrote:

> [2]In this blest quietness clamorings cease;
> Here in thy presence dwells infinite
> peace.
> Yonder the strife and cry, yonder the sin.
> Lord, I have shut the door; thou art
> within.

Not only do periods of silence rest the soul, but the body as well. Many times I have observed that as I become still before the Lord, I feel his presence coming over my body, loosening tense muscles and bringing physical relaxation.

4. DETACHMENT

One of the later results of waiting on God will be a certain sense of detachment. People who are unhappy because their mate does not love them enough, or their children neglect them, or friends at church don't pay enough attention will become less and less dependent on others for happiness. They will become increasingly drawn to the person of Jesus—so much so that all else loses the strength of its former attraction.

Not only will we become more detached from people but also from material things. We will become less "cumbered about much serving," and less "careful and troubled about many things."

(Ref. Luke 10:40-41)

What follows this detachment is a much more simple lifestyle.

A. W. Tozer said:

> [3]We Christians must simplify our lives or
> lose untold treasures on earth and in
> eternity.

Because of the prize set before us, we gladly
strip ourselves of encumbrances which impede our
spiritual progress. We become more content with
such things as we have and lose excessive interest
in striving after more, because we already have all
we need in Jesus.

5. STRENGTH

Two familiar passages on being still are Isaiah
40:31- and 30:-15-:

> But they that wait upon the Lord shall
> renew *their* strength; . . .
> . . . in quietness and in confidence shall
> be your strength: . . .

The term, *a weak Christian,* could not be ap-
plied to one who communes with God. Something
happens to his backbone and he is able to stand up
straight and be:

> . . . strong in the Lord and in the power
> of his might.   (Eph. 6:-10)

A friend who was undergoing the trauma of a
divorce found release as she stopped her agonized
praying and sat at the feet of Jesus. A deep and
loving relationship developed which enabled her to
joyfully triumph in Christ.

I also discovered that when I stopped yearning
for earthly happiness and learned to be satisfied

with Jesus that I seemed to stand up inside. I was no longer a craven creature begging for crumbs of attention from human beings, but felt as though I were indeed:

> The King's daughter . . . all glorious
> within: . . .   (Psalm 45:13-)

6. FRUITFULNESS

One objection raised by those who do not understand the value of times of silence is that it makes one spiritually lazy, self-centered, impractical. This, of course, is not at all true. Those who are closest to God are most willing to serve Him, and generally they are the ones the pastor can most depend upon for various services in the church.

7. LIVING IN HIS PRESENCE

We begin by spending a little time daily being still. As we progress we often increase the length of time we do so and we also learn to take moments during the day. Eventually, we can begin to "live and move and have our being" in Him. (Ref. Acts 17:28)

This does not necessarily mean that every moment we are communing, but that much of the time we are doing so.

In *Practice Of The Presence Of God,* Brother Lawrence says:

> [4]And I make it my business only to persevere in His holy presence, wherein I keep myself by a simple attention and general fond regard to God, which I may call an actual presence of God; or to speak

better, an habitual, silent and secret
conversation of the soul with God. It
often causes me joys and raptures inwardly, and sometimes also outwardly,
so great that I am forced to use means to
moderate them and prevent their ap-
pearance to others.

He also says:

[5]My most useful method is this simple attention and such a general regard to
God, to whom I find myself often at-
tached with greater sweetness and
delight than of an infant at her mother's
breast; so that if I dare use the expression, I should choose to call this state the
bosom of God for the inexpressible
sweetness which I taste and experience
there.

8. TRANSFORMATION

But we all, with open face beholding as
in a glass the glory of the Lord, are
changed [Weymouth: transformed] into
the same image from glory to glory, *even*
as by the Spirit of the Lord. (2 Cor. 3:18)

Much of what has been said regarding the
blessings of sitting still before the Lord make it
seem all bliss. However, the Lord is interested not
only in making us **feel** good but also to **be** good. He
knows that the sin and self life embedded within us
are obstacles to fullest rapport and union with Him.
And so begins the often painful process of cleansing
which enables us to see the Lord more clearly.

The Scripture says:

> Blessed *are* the pure in heart: for they
> shall see God.   (Matt. 5:8)

And the purer our hearts become the clearer
will be out sight of Him.

9. HELP IN TIMES OF TRIAL

Often when I am so troubled that I really don't
know how to pray, I sit still in his presence, not
saying anything, just being with Him. In the song
by William Cashing, *Hiding In Thee,* he said:

> How often when trials like sea billows
> roll,
> Have I hidden in Thee O thou rock of my
> soul.

And this is what happens when we wait on God.

10. KNOWLEDGE OF GOD

Psalm 46:10- tells us to:

> Be still and know that I *am* God: . . .

This seemingly simple Scripture encompasses
every degree of the knowledge of God—from that of
the new Christian who truthfully says, "I know the
Lord," to that of the mature saint who knows God
in depth.

We can know God through seeing Him and His
ways in Scripture; we can also know Him in our
soul, but as we grow in communion we progress
beyond mind and soul into the deepest part of our
being, which is spirit.

There is no stopping place in the knowledge of God. Years after his conversion, when St. Paul was a mature saint, he still cried:

> That I may know Him, . . .   (Phil. 3:10-)

Whatever degree of the knowledge of God we individually attain will be greatly enhanced by the amount of time we spend with Him.

As A. W. Tozer said:

> [6]God can be known satisfactorily only as we devote time to Him.

One thing we can be sure of—the longer we know Him the more we love him. This perhaps is the sweetest and best of all results of waiting on God. Nothing else brings such joy, such contentment, such fulfillment as being in love with God.

Chapter 17
Summing It All Up

We were not made for Time.
We were made for Eternity.

When God made man, it was with the express purpose of having someone like unto Himself with whom He could have intimate and loving fellowship. It was to be a reciprocal love. Through the history of His association with man, His purposes remain the same.

From generation to generation His eyes run to and fro throughout the whole earth to find a man whose heart is perfect toward Him. Through the Holy Spirit He constantly seeks man and woos him unto Himself. Wherever He finds one who responds, He lavishes upon that one His love— limited only by the capacity of that person to receive it.

The average Christian is seeking God's favor instead of His face. He wants answers to prayer, power, strength for service, help in problems. All of these are legitimate motives for seeking God.

But how many like David will cry,

> One *thing* have I desired of the Lord,
> that will I seek after; that I may dwell in
> the house of the Lord all the days of my
> life, to behold the beauty of the Lord,
> and to enquire in His temple.
>
> (Psalm 27:4)

Even though David was busy fighting battles and winning victories for the Lord, he took time for prayer and praise and stillness. Despite his personal human weaknesses he was called: "a man after God's own heart." Chiefly because he was so devoted to the Lord that he took time to behold God's face in communion with Him.

(Ref. 1 Sam. 13:14 & Acts 13:22)

It is such as these that God is desiring.

Then why does God seek those who will love Him with all the heart, soul, mind and strength, and who will give themselves wholly to Him? Why does He long to deepen and strengthen that relationship when He finds it? What motivates God?

Is it just for the comparatively fleeting joy of His fellowship with that man or woman during their brief sojourn **on earth**? Is it possible that God may have a much larger purpose than this—one that extends beyond what man shall be and do on earth? Would not God desire to develop on earth capacities in His children which will be extended through all eternity—capacities not only to serve Him in heaven, but also to fellowship Him in the highest degrees of love and intimacy?

To properly appraise the value of the practice of silent prayer, we must place it within the context of the whole purpose and meaning of life on earth. I believe that silent communion will do more toward preparing one for the fullest enjoyment and participation in heaven than almost any other spiritual exercise. True, we will not be idle in heaven, for,

> . . . His servants shall serve Him:
> (Rev. 22:-3)

But we must remember that the primary relationship of each individual Christian to Jesus in heaven will be that of love. On earth the church is called *the bride* and Jesus *the Bridegroom.* In heaven it will be the same. Therefore God seeks those who will spend enough time with Him on earth to develop a capacity for a deep love relationship and ability to respond to Him in the fullest degree. He is seeking out such a people to be His special treasure.

His Son Jesus invites us, "Come unto Me, sit at My feet, be with Me. Learn to love Me and enjoy Me. Let Me bestow upon you My love, My joy, My tranquility, My holiness."

He calls to the divorced, the widow, the single man and woman, the deformed, the poor, the outcasts of society, "Come, find happiness and fulfillment in Me."

He invites the homosexual, the lesbian, "Come, sit at My feet; let Me pour My holy love into you; let Me make the crooked places straight; let me fill those empty places."

He also invites the normal, the well-adjusted, the wealthy, the happy: "Come, sit in My presence, for in My presence is fullness of joy. Set your mind, your affections, your heart upon Me."

He invites all, "Take time to be still. Let Me shape you into a vessel, not for time alone, but for Eternity.

Be still and know that I am God. Be still, be still, be still. . . ."

Chapter 18
Personal Testimony

... ye are complete in Him, ...
      (Col. 2:-10- KJV)

... you have come to fulness of life in
Him, ...   (RSV)

*... you have everything when you have
Christ, ...*   (LB)

In the first chapter I related how through silent communion I began a beautiful love relationship with Jesus which transformed my Christian life.

Some time later another romance began, this time in the natural, when I met my husband. During the early years of marriage I was very happy, both in the love of Jesus and in my role as wife and later, mother.

I faithfully maintained my daily habit of an hour or more of Bible and prayer. I was active in Christian service in church, Sunday school and writing. Because my love for Jesus had been so strong, perhaps I began to take it for granted; so I gradually became less diligent about keeping the love-trysts with Jesus. By the end of 23 years of marriage, silent communion was no longer an important part of my life.

Then my husband died. During the following months that hateful specter of loneliness began peering into my window again. The first year of widowhood was a struggle with grief; the second, a time of forgetting and the third year I began experiencing a longing for human companionship.

Although this is a normal reaction, still I considered it as a low period in my Christian experience. I felt disappointed in myself because I had once known that "Love divine, all loves excelling," which had made me so "complete in Him."

How could I have regressed to the state where I could no longer say that Jesus is all I need. What happened to my love for Him? As I examined my heart, I realized that *that love* was still there, but the flame was burning very low. So I began again to take time, along with my regular devotions, to just sit at Jesus' feet, look into His face and remember "the day of our espousals."

This time communion was quite different.

When I first began, many years ago, I knew nothing of how to proceed or what to expect. All I had were three books and simple, basic instructions from several of His lovers. At that time it took about a year and more, an hour or so daily, to finally learn how to stay my mind on Jesus and to eventually fall in love with Him.

Now as I began again, it took only a few months for the flame to be rekindled, and it has been burning brightly ever since.

During the course of my renewed waiting on God I read the lives of other lovers of God. Here I learned in detail their experiences and methods, their sacrifices and their attainments.

I rejoiced with Francis of Assissi in his deep love of Jesus; I suffered with Teresa of Avila at the price she gladly paid to enter into the depths of union with God; I longed after the abiding life of Brother Lawrence and I responded to the call of inwardness in the books of Andrew Murray and A. W. Tozer.

I was inspired at reading of the depths of the knowledge of God and the love of Jesus which these men and women had achieved. And I felt humbled at the feet of spiritual giants who had suffered the loss of all things and counted them but refuse that they might attain their goal of union with Christ and lovership with Him.

As I continue to sit at the feet of Jesus in silent worship I now do so in an entirely different context. I know much more of the methods, obstacles, goals. It is easier to be still and know that He is God. Often I simply close my eyes, wait on Him just a short time and I feel His presence and power quickly. At times He manifests Himself in an overwhelming sense of His presence.

I still have dryness and distracting thoughts. But I realize from past experience that despite this, something is happening at a deeper level, where spirit meets Spirit—in that deep and holy place within. I find Him changing me, making me more careful about my life and relationships with people, so that there is no cloud between God and my soul.

In times of strain and testing, I know no greater refuge and comfort than to nestle in the arms of Jesus.

I have also learned the delights of sharing together with Him the joys of life—family, friends, woods and parks. Human and natural joys are enhanced because of Jesus' presence.

But always I must say in the end, with Bernard of Clairvaux's *Jesus, Thou Joy Of Loving Hearts:*

> From the best bliss that earth imparts,
> we turn unfilled to Thee again.

Jesus always maintains His position as THE FAIREST OF THEM ALL.

Never have I been more content, more peaceful, more fulfilled than I am now.

However, I am not sitting in an ivory tower enjoying my fellowship with Jesus and letting the rest of the world go by. I have never been so busy for God, nor so fruitful.

Yes, I am my Beloved's and He is mine. He is all I need. I do not say it by faith; I say it by experience. He has made me so happy that my prayer for every lonely, sad and needy person is that he would sit at the feet of Jesus long enough and often enough to discover the wonders of His love and the beauty of His person.

For this reason is this book written.

SCRIPTURES ON SILENCE

And Isaac went out to meditate in the field at eventide . . .   (Gen. 24:63-)

And after the earthquake a fire; but the Lord was not in the fire; and after the fire a still small voice. And it was so when Elijah heard it that he wrapped his face in his mantle and went out and stood in the entering in of the cave. And behold, there came a voice unto him and said, "What doest thou here, Elijah?"   (1 Kings 19:12-13)

Stand in awe and sin not; commune with your own heart upon your bed and be still.   (Psalm 4:4)

He maketh me to lie down in green pastures; he leadeth me beside the still waters. (Hebrew: *waters of quietness*)   (Psalm 23:2)

Rest in the Lord (Hebrew: *be silent to*) and wait patiently for him . . .   (Psalm 37:7-)

I waited patiently for the Lord; (Hebrew: *in waiting I waited*) and he inclined unto me and heard my cry.   (Psalm 40:1)

BE STILL AND KNOW THAT I *AM* GOD: . . .
                                          (Psalm 46:10-)

Truly my soul waiteth (Hebrew: *is silent*) upon God: from him *cometh* my salvation.   (Psalm 62:1)

When I remember thee upon my bed, *and* meditate on thee in the *night* watches. (Psalm 63:6)

Praise waiteth (Hebrew: *is silent*) for thee, O God, in Sion: and unto thee shall the vow be performed: (Psalm 65:1)

My meditation of him shall be sweet: I will be glad in the Lord.   (Psalm 104:34)

Unto thee lift I up mine eyes, O thou that dwellest in the heavens.
Behold, as the eyes of servants *look* unto the hand of their masters, *and* as the eyes of a maiden unto the hand of her mistress; so our eyes *wait* upon the Lord our God, until that he have mercy upon us.
(Psalm 123:1-2)

I wait for the Lord, my soul doth wait, and in his word do I hope.
My soul *waiteth* for the Lord more than they that watch for the momming . . .   (Psalm 130:5-6-)

Lord, my heart is not haughty, nor mine eyes lofty: neither do I exercise myself in great matters, or in things too high for me.
Surely I have behaved and quieted myself, (Hebrew: *my soul*) as a child that is weaned of his mother; my soul *is* even as a weaned child.
Let Israel hope in the Lord from henceforth and for ever.   (Psalm 131:1-3)

The whole earth is at rest, *and* is quiet: they break forth into singing.   (Isaiah 14:7)

Thou wilt keep *him* in perfect peace, *whose* mind (margin: thoughts or imagination) is stayed *on thee:* because he trusteth in thee.   (Isaiah 26:3)

For the Egyptians shall help in vain, and to no purpose: therefore have I cried concerning this, Their strength *is* to sit still.   (Isaiah 30:7)

For thus saith the Lord God, the Holy One of Israel; In returning and rest shall ye be saved; in quietness and in confidence shall be your strength: and ye would not.
But ye said, No; for we will flee upon horses; therefore shall ye flee: and, We will ride upon the swift; therefore shall they that pursue you be swift.
(Isaiah 30:15-16)

And the work of righteousness shall be peace; and the effect of righteousness quietness and assurance for ever.
And my people shall dwell in a peaceable habitation, and in sure dwellings, and in quiet resting places;   (Isaiah 32:17-18)

But they that wait upon the LORD shall renew *their* strength; they shall mount up with wings as eagles; they shall run, and not be weary; *and* they shall walk, and not faint.   (Isaiah 40:31)

For since the beginning of the world *men* have not heard, nor perceived by the ear, neither hath the eye seen, O God, beside thee, *what* he hath prepared for him that waiteth for him.

(Isaiah 64:4)

The LORD *is* good unto them that wait for him, to the soul *that* seeketh him.
It is good that *a man* should both hope and quietly wait for the salvation of the LORD.   (Lam. 3:25-26)

Therefore turn thou to thy God: keep mercy and judgment, and wait on thy God continually.

(Hosea 12:6)

But the LORD *is* in his holy temple: LET ALL THE EARTH KEEP SILENCE BEFORE HIM.
(Habakkuk 2:20)

BE SILENT, O ALL FLESH, BEFORE THE LORD: FOR HE IS RAISED UP OUT OF HIS HOLY HABITATION.   (Zechariah 2:13)

Come unto me, all *ye* that labour and are heavy laden, and I will give you rest.
Take my yoke upon you, and learn of me; for I am meek and lowly in heart: and ye shall find rest unto your souls.   (St. Matthew 11:28-29)

Now it came to pass, as they went, that he entered into a certain village: and a certain woman named Martha received him into her house.
And she had a sister called Mary, which ALSO SAT AT JESUS' FEET, AND HEARD HIS WORD.

But Martha was cumbered about much serving, and came to him, and said, Lord, dost thou not care that my sister hath left me to serve alone? bid her therefore that she help me.
And Jesus answered and said unto her, Martha, Martha, thou art careful and troubled about many things:
But one thing is needful: and Mary hath chosen that good part, which shall not be taken away from her. (St. Luke 10:38-42)

Now there was leaning on Jesus' bosom one of his disciples, whom Jesus loved. (St. John 13:23)

But we all, with open face beholding as in a glass the glory of the Lord, are changed into the same image from glory to glory, *even* as by the Spirit of the Lord. (2 Corinthians 3:18)

And that ye study to be quiet, and to do your own business, and to work with your own hands, as we commanded you; (1 Thessalonians 4:11)

Now them that are such we command and exhort by our Lord Jesus Christ, that with quietness they work, and eat their own bread.
(2 Thessalonians 3:12)

I exhort therefore, that, first of all, supplications, prayers, intercessions, *and* giving of thanks, be made for all men;
For kings, and *for* all that are in authority; that we may lead a quiet and peaceable life in all godliness and honesty. (1 Timothy 2:1-2)

Whose adorning let it not be that outward *adorning* of plaiting the hair, and of wearing of gold, or of putting on of apparel;
But *let it be* the hidden man of the heart, in that which is not corruptible, *even the ornament* of a meek and quiet spirit, which is in the sight of God of great price.   (1 Peter 3:3-4)

And when he had opened the seventh seal, THERE WAS SILENCE IN HEAVEN ABOUT THE SPACE OF HALF AN HOUR.   (Revelation 8:1)

REFERENCES (BIBLIOGRAPHY)

Page xi

Taken from *The Root of the Righteous*, by A. W. Tozer, Christian Publications, Inc., Harrisburg, PA, 1955 page 145. Used by permission.

CHAPTER 1

Entire first chapter is an article by Anne Sandberg printed in *Aglow Magazine's* fall issue, 1975, pages 28-31. Abridged.

Permission to use granted by the *Aglow Magazine*, Edmonds, WN 98020.

CHAPTER 2

1. Song, *Jesus, I Am Resting*, Jean Pigott, Public Domain.

2. Song, *Jesus, the Very Thought of Thee*, Bernard of Clairvaux, Public Domain.

CHAPTERS 3 & 4

1. Song, *Near to the Heart of God*, C. B. McAfee, Public Domain.

CHAPTER 6

1. *Of God and Men*, A. W. Tozer, 1960, page 106, Christian Publications, Inc., Harrisburg, PA 17101. Used by permission.

CHAPTER 7

1. Scripture text from Good News Bible, Old Testament. Copyright © 1976 American Bible Society. Used by permission.

2. Scripture Text TAB, the Amplified Bible, Old Testament. Copyright © 1962, 1964, by Zondervan Publishing House, Grand Rapids, MI. Used by pemission.

3. Song, *Blessed Quietness*, Manie P. Ferguson, Public Domain.

CHAPTER 8

1. *The Power of Stillness*, an article by A. B. Simpson. Used by permission of Christian Publications, Inc. Ibid. This was taken from an article in a Sunday school paper. Christian Publications was unable to locate the source of this quote, but gave permission to use it as is.

CHAPTER 9

1. *Waiting on God,* by Andrew Murray, page 63. No date given. Fleming H. Revell Co., Old Tappan, NJ 07675. Used by permission.

2. *Letters By A Modern Mystic,* Frank Laubach, page 45. Laubach Literacy Int'l. National Affiliation for Literacy Advancement. New Readers Press, Syracuse, NY 13210. By permission.

CHAPTER 10

1. *Radiant Glory,* by G. P. Gardiner, pages 150-151 (re Mrs. Martha Robinson) Bread of Life, Brooklyn, NY © 1962. By permission.

2. *Waitng on God,* by Andrew Murray, pages 120-121. Ibid.

CHAPTER 11

1. *Talkativeness,* tract. Author unknown. Used by permission of publisher, Christian Triumph Co., Corpus Cristi, TX 78405.

CHAPTEP- 13

1. Song, *Lord, I Have Shut the Door,* by Wm. M. Runyan. Hope Publishing Co., owner. All rights reserved. Used by special permission. Hope Publishing Co., Carol Stream, IL.

2. *Open Heart, Open Home,* by Karen Mains, pages 192-193. David C. Cook Publishing Co., Elgin, IL. Used by permission.

3. Quote from letter. Used by permission.

CHAPTER 14

1. *Waiting on God,* by Andrew Murray, page 98, Ibid.

2. Song, *Jesus, Thou Joy of Loving Hearts,* Bernard of Clairvaux, Public Domain.

3. *The Game With Minutes,* by Frank Laubach, page 25. Ibid.

CHAPTER 15

1. *Letters By A Modern Mystic,* by Frank Laubach, page 33. Ibid.

2. *Waiting on God,* by Andrew Marray, page 48. Ibid.

CHAPTER 16

1. Song, *Draw Me Nearer,* Fanny Crosby, Public Domain.

2. *Lord, I Have Shut the Door,* by Wm. M. Runyan, Ibid.

3. *Of God and Men,* by A. W. Tozer, 1960, page 103. Ibid.

4. *The Practice of the Presence of God*, by Bro. Lawrence, page 36. Fleming H. Revel Co., Old Tapan, NJ. Used by permission.

5. *The Practice of the Presence of God*, page 37. Ibid.

6. *The Root of the Righteous*, by A. W. Tozer, page 12. Ibid.

BOOK ORDER FORM

COPY THIS PAGE AND USE IT AS AN ORDER FORM FOR ADDITIONAL COPIES OF THIS BOOK.

Copies	Qty. Ordered	Price	Sub-Total
1 - 4	_____	X $7.95 each =	$ _____
5 - 10	_____	X $6.95 each =	$ _____
11 - plus	_____	X $5.95 each =	$ _____
For shipping cost add:		X $0.50 each =	$ _____
		Total =	**$ _____**

Please send your order to:

Martha Jacobson Bauer
9818 Estrella Drive
Spring Valley, CA 91977

Please send me _____ copies of this book:

A TIME TO BE SILENT

Please send BOOKS to: *(PleaseType or Print)*

Name: ....

Address: ....

City: ....

State.....................Zip..

Enclosed is my check in the amount of $

NOTE, by Martha Jacobson Bauer, (Author of *Hey, This Is Fun!*): If Jesus tarries, I hope to sell enough books to pay the expense of printing, then give away several thousand to my brothers and sisters in Nigeria, plus a thousand or two to other missionaries. In fact, every church should have it in its library.

My first book, *HEY, THIS IS FUN!*, is also available from me for the same prices (per above ORDER FORM). It is full of adventure and Christian victory from my 40 years missionary ministry in Nigeria, West Africa. It will help make missionaries out of your young people. It, too, should be in every library.